Ambrosia Sides

Poems

About the Book

Poetry is soul nourishing. And of course, there is a need for it as much as need for salt in the food. Ambrosia sides is meant to be just that—something on the side, a flavoursome mouthful. The Gods may sometimes crave some pickle on the side too.

The poems in this book are free-flowing compositions. And while they are diverse in themes, they have been categorised into the Trinity construct—Brahma, the deity of creation where all things begin; Vishnu, the deity of preservation where desire fuels preservation and Shiva, the deity of destruction, where endings prevail.

Ambrosia Sides

Poems

Abhijita Kulshrestha

SHAKTI BOOKS
An Imprint of Har-Anand Publications Pvt Ltd

Published by Ashok Gosain and Ashish Gosain for
HAR-ANAND PUBLICATIONS PVT LTD
E-49/3, Okhla Industrial Area, Phase-II, New Delhi-110020
Tel: 41603490
E-mail: info@haranandbooks.com/haranand@rediffmail.com
Shop online at: www.haranandbooks.com

Reprint, 2020

Printed in India

Shakti Books

Shakti Books is a significant series devoted to representing the range of issues pertaining to gender and its overlapping and intersectional concerns and contexts. It is unique in its ability to connect with well-known scholars writing on gender issues as well as to reach out to bright young talents negotiating and mediating the field.

The series seeks to analyse the patriarchal structures and institutions at play and strives to engage with history, culture, socio-economic order and the political nuances of the same. It focuses on the 'invisible,' the 'unspoken' and the 'new' within the field of gender studies.

While writings on gender are available across disciplines or within scholarly readership, the interrogation of gender in this series is refreshing and cutting edge. It undertakes to sensitize its readers to unravel the nuances of gender in the everyday and encourages them to take part in this conversation.

The series has a multidisciplinary outlook interlinking literature, science, economics, history, sociology, culture, arts, aesthetics, religion, politics, geography, media and education. The range of issues include class, caste, religion, race, ethnicity, region, language, age, desire and sexuality and their intersecting and overlapping concerns with gender. The series focuses on women of today, both in the urban and rural contexts, who are aspirational and building on the gains of a sustained women's movement in India.

In a systematic and accessible manner, *Shakti Books* makes refined and sophisticated links to the widespread network of gender studies which includes the creative, critical, communicative, cultural and the contemporary. The emphasis of the series is to examine the perceptions of gender in the present, its link to the historical past and its significance for the contemporary times. *Shakti Books* has been the first series to consider and address these critical connections and provide a wide platform to a range of young authors and scholars to bring forward their writings on gender issues. It reiterates the indispensability of gender equality and focuses on aspects of the complexity of gender through incisive analysis of the same.

Bijayalaxmi Nanda
General Editor

Foreword

Ambrosia Sides is a rich collection of poems which is not bound by any rigid form. The churning of the ocean of life brings forth the nectar to sustain it. Similarly Abhijita Kulshrestha has brought in the elements of myth and mystique to nourish one's soul with her poetic vision. The predominant metaphors in her poems – creation, preservation and destruction – are reflected in the three thematic divisions in the collection. The aptly titled themes after the Hindu Holy Trinity of Brahma, Vishnu and Shiva provide an interesting depth to the collection.

The poems combine the mystical and esoteric with social and personal experiences. In the poem 'Embattled' she writes lyrically:

Sleep is kind, dreams have dissolved
Wondrous silence, I have been absolved.

The beauty of these lines reflects a magic realism similar to the work of the great Colombian novelist Gabriel Garcia Marquez.

There is also an undercurrent of recognising the inner turmoil of a woman's heart. A perennial question of identity.... Of finding herself. In the poem 'Circle' she says

Trepidation
Upon my turn
What shall I find
After I return?

Abhijita Kulshrestha's poems are musical notes in words. They have a unique sense of rhythm and reason. They are evocative and thus draw the reader into using their own imagination to find the resonance of the spiritual ethos present in them.

The essence of this collection is best summed in the poet's own words:

Yes I must write
I must do it right.

And she has done it right – multihued collection encompassing the spiritual, the human and the magical in a holistic manner. The poems will bring succour to poetry lovers in the same way as nectar nourishes human life.

BIJAYALAXMI NANDA

Contents

I

II

III

To the shy gossamer Muse
Inspiring a gushing spring ...

I

Brahma

What do you do, O Brahma
With extra clay

After creating
Your heart's desire

The leftovers
Sticking to human moulds?

Gumption

A dandelion seed
Slave to the breeze

Intoxicated by the possibility
Agrees to ride the current

Unseen river
Of fated path

Offers the waif, a fleeting lift
Before its burial

To come alive
And dream again

River Red

In my womb
A drumbeat reigns
A clap of thunder
And gypsy dance begins

Some red, some earth
I must take rebirth
A wild calling, to unbelong
Has somehow become my heart song

Don't be sad and don't you cry
I'm not saying a goodbye
It's only my baptism
A folded love note

I must gather it from the earth's throat
She anoints my courage lava red

Oh she's proud and impressed
What a daughter she has bred

And as I flow
True to myself
I welcome you
To River Red!

Discovery

In pages of a book
I found you by chance

A mirror lay hidden
Amid a wordy trance

Animus
Magnanimous

I have found me
Indeed, a serendipitous discovery

My right side breathes
A rich life it weaves

The left, is now free you see
For now, forevermore *'left'* it cannot be!

An Unborn Daughter's Petition

Mother, to forgive myself
I must take birth
And so I can be born
You must turn earth

I am asking too much
You must come ready mother
A simple touch
Inside this shell, I wait

I wait to be born
Hunger scorches my insides
Only you can lead me to redemption
You know the path to where love hides

So let your sinews build into mine
Let your heart give me a beat divine
You must help me forgive myself mother
You are my only path, no other...

Faith

I ring the bell
Blow a conch shell
Sing fire-lit hymns
Even though my own light dims

A litany of desires
Of carnal fires
In marshes of greed
Of Satan's creed

I swim, I float
On a hopeful note
I've heard in the eyes
Of my addictive vice

In the curls and the whorls
Is mystic surrender
I will come to your rescue
Cast yourself asunder

Purpose

Yes, I must write,
I must do it right

When the last train whistles in dead of the night
Unspoken words and untold stories in my belly, rise

The ghosts of memories,
These wily fireflies

When I am the galaxy, and I am the worlds
It's only words I have, these Stygian pearls

Undoing the misery
Unravelling the whorls

Until day breaks, until the touch of light
Unfinished business, untouched by fire

The night's ceramic dreams
Crumbling with unfulfilled desire.

Voices

No, it did not happen
I am sure of my sight
They told me I was a brave girl
I would have put up a fight

Until you came along
And flung a stone in the dirt
I wouldn't have really known
Where it actually hurt

So thank you for making a leery pass
That sick catcall, the whistle
For when you served it under my nose
I was ready to bristle

Could ignore it no more, nor pretend or hide
The ignominy is yours, now that I have defied

Shame for my gender and your pride justified?
The coin is flipped - you should be petrified.

Looking Away

Paints and pens
Pants and pains

Slip of the cup
Cups the slip

Thin refrains of protest
Yet he doesn't refrain

Wails get lost
In veiled meanings

Embattled

Heat wave, cold feet
Warm tears, take to the streets

Beat spirit, calloused soul
Shallow breath, tastes foul

Self-loathing, desire to die
Has taken over, the will to fly

Dark night, shadows follow
This pain, can't swallow

The cliff nears, the void howls
I will leap, into the jowls

Sleep is kind, dreams have dissolved
Wondrous silence, I have been absolved

Hearth

Those who sing of togetherness
Kindred spirits in unison

Began separately at different times
But today they stand as one

Different stories filling their handbags
Different keys jangling in a bunch

Sisterhood seals a covenant
These are witches you can't hunt

They chant, they sway
And utter a spell

In their midst you find a home
Until it's all well, until all is well…

Balm

Dull aches
Gave way to tarred roads
Each time
Hurt drove me out
I came back, yet again
With armload of bags

A new scarf to hide my shame,
A new blouse to drape a heartache,
New pants for a stifling morality
New bags for more baggage

But today I have returned
With loaded verse
A clean head
And some pilfered blue sky in my pockets

Circles

Doorknobs,
Bends in the road,
Pages of a book,
I lie in bed

Trepidation…
Upon my turn
What shall I find
After I return?

Jail Break

Through tight muscle strands of my heart
Words strain
Struggling to come out
But these bars, they are hard to bend

Core

Who knew
Music slept
Dormant
In metal wire
Until pulled taut
And plucked

Who knew
Notes hide
In bamboo's belly
Offering themselves
Only to the sweetest caress
Of knower's lips

Who knew
Force of words

That wait behind
Floodgates of the heart
Only to run amok
In silent rooms

II

Vishnu

The Sun's rays
Offering golden dregs

Of your essence
My sustenance

Do you stand behind the Sun, O Vishnu
And extend his hand?

Quest

China heart
Your porcelain insides
Long stained, with ancient love
Interest no longer
Gaze of the tourist
Searching for a steal
In the alcoves of old street
Not knowing, it's his home
He's no tourist.

A Wisp

How can I tell you of my love
No Greek alphabet to fathom its antiquity
No anchor dropped to plumb the depths
It's a mystery that roams the nights
Singing to fireflies
Beneath a scarlet moon

Rush

A metallic two step
A quick pirouette
On the notebook
A liquid word
Hasty, reckless
Sealing itself dry
An identity
Etching itself
Proudly
Writing this history
Of my heart

Outlaws

Fragrant jasmine
Lying languid
Amid loose curls
Sometimes rebellious
Led by rapscallion wind

Savouring adventure
Racing in quick sands
Weightless rascals
Name-dropping perfumed notes
Every now and then

You let them stay
Yet you let them stay...

Allure

Come with me, I say nervously
I have rehearsed several versions

Charm, plead, seduce
Pray, trade, obstruce
Yet as I speak, elemental I turn
Basic is my form, it is where I return

Star seed you are
Galactic dust I am

Come with me
Let's dream up a dream

With love's dewy mist
We could rend stellar magic unbound

Snap

Even if I write
It doesn't go away

Salty memory
Of tears kissed

The crisp break
Of a pretzel heart

Twister

The fleeting strains of love
Have called my name

A soft spell beckons
Every night, as I dream

Valleys echo misty eyed
Brooks gurgle, doves cry

As your lips moon-stain mine
With silvery dew from a faraway sky

Tides

Every full moon
My womb aches
The dull throb
Reaches the heart
Slips into the soul
And becomes a hunger
The kind that makes the wolf howl

To the Cosmic Twin

You are more than what I am
Jealous eyes claim

Could I be you… like you, at least
Question stuck in my throat, stifled roar of a beast

A free spirit - unfettered you roam
You climb the tree of childhood home

With joyous laughter bubbling over
While I peer from underneath the cover

I watch, looking up envious and glum
You pluck and bite – ah, the ripeness of a June plum

Sister, was it the same place from where we had come?
Will you share your secret, please some...

I look downward to the ground
Turn and walk in without a sound

The door, the home that held us both
Was suddenly womb I needed the most

To wait my turn and incubate
Till the seed of joy can germinate.

Caught

I try to create
Even meditate

The thought of your hands
Touching me, firebrands

They invade this landscape
There is no escape

I linger for a bit and move away from the easel
Pop! goes the weasel ...

Why

One thousand questions
Unanswered

One strand of faith
Unbroken

One skewed balance
Yet I walk

The tightrope
Of life

Art

It was a new night
The rules had fled

In the realm of irreverence
Words just flew

From tip of the nib
Keystroke to keystroke

From muse to the artist
Needle to skin

For now there's peace
The heart is all sewed up

Resting on soft blanket
Of anaesthetised dreams

The Wait

Time keeper
If you could rummage,
In your memory vault

Is there a gift
Marked with my name
To be delivered in this life?

Warp and Weft

I weave
Through crowds

I weave
Through nights

I weave
Through words

Even though they stall
Despite the dark
Past the slipperiness

This fabric of my dreams
This alchemy of wanting
This magic of love

Mutiny

Delicious amber
Melts and trickles down

Oh! It's burning your skin
It will leave scars

It was meant to slake
It was supposed to bejewel

Look now,
The waywardness of desire

Amends

In your face, Krishna
Traces of my past I see

Two broken links
Resisting the magnetic pull

Fearing the pinch,
hammering and twisting

The unkind silversmith though,
Can make us whole again

Orbit

A jar of moonlight
Knocked over by a sigh

Spilled across the skies
A runaway silvery stain

Tracing a path
From your star to mine

Dream

Salmon of desire
Swims upstream

As I lie
caressing your hair

Robust pink
Or almost coral

A passion
hard to describe

And then
I am awake

Monsoons

Old boats
Moored at clunky harbours

Old tides
Repeatedly have a run in

Old salty memories
Mark these moisture laden days

III

Shiva

His blue throat
A rich impression

That centres on the forehead
A giant luminescent stamp, a vision

Another life
Another planet

Another pantheon
Another kingdom

Am I the Shiva
Am I the *tat-tvam*?

Time

Clocking the miles
Wave upon wave
There is a rhythm
But of alien arithmetic

Sometimes it is all sea
Sometimes the shore, I see

Wave upon wave
As I crash into the rocks
As I lie awash on the sands
As I retreat into the liquid beyond

I am a million fragments
I am the sea
I am the pieces
I am the whole

Separation

The snow falls noiselessly
On warm, pulsating hearts
Feathery death wish
A cold cleaver, unfeeling ice...

Futility

Fingers hesitate
To resuscitate
Gasping words
Bleeding incoherent
Moody paper
Dissolves in falling rain...

Riot

This silence
Is heavy
Noises of the head crowd it
Two aching hearts
Goading two stubborn minds
To grab the sheet
On this marriage bed

Pell-Mell

There's a stampede
A riot of words

Ink stains
Purple plains

Papyrus moors
Turn battleground

Ideas
Unwilling to be found

Mind Bender

What if
The mountain peaks gave in
Collapsing under a psychic weight

What if
The ocean boiled over
With an unheard of rage

What if
The wind just sat down
Travel weary and tired

What if
The fire in belly
Felt low and refused to ignite

What if
The skies had trouble holding up
And simply wanted to die...

Rage

Thunder rose
At the base of throat

Suffocating softness
It grew red

Dragon's breath
You wretched wretch

Crushing punch
Collapsing lungs

Hungry death
Does cunning math

Why settle for one
When there's Devils run

Let's choke it while
It's still dragon's breath

Contrast

Snow crunching under feet
Crystal beads of arctic desire

She bends to pick them
They melt at a mere touch

She thinks she ruined their existence for wonderment
They martyr themselves to a sensation of warmth

A vast white phenomenon
Versus a mirage

Mystery

Five hundred friends
Five fingers to hold

One hundred secrets
A little heart,behold

Half journeys shared
Halves untold

Stuckness

You gaze long into the abyss,
The abyss gazes back into you

Tired, he looked up
Diverted his gaze

Couldn't get past the grief
Of *et tu*

Threat

There is a void
Screaming

Trailing everywhere you go
Tugging at shirt tails

You hear it louder
You fear it more

You have been leaping chasms longer than you know
This void is afraid

Of the fire in your eyes
Of the waters of your crystal being

If they turn on it
This void will go

Dissolving, dismembering
you and me - as we know...

Winter

Perfectly empty evening
With hollow eyes
Stares
At chimney smoke

And then turns the gaze
At fading gray mountain
Loss will be complete
Soon

The cicadas will confirm
When it is dark
In an alien language
To a shrivelled heart

Heartbreak

It's a good sized hollow, a sphere
Goes right through me
I carry it around

Somewhere near the heart
Where your finger traced my name
A fair percentage of my being

Help me remember
How it came about
This black hole in my universe

Vagabond

I have paid
All the *I Owe You's*

With my sleep
And dreams

Dreams in which
I curl up right into your arms

Closure

As you lie
Grieving
Lamenting my absence

Take a moment
Feel
My freedom

About the Author

A poet's soul simply is. You can't kill it hide it or shame it away. It will string and weave. One dons many hats but it sits within silently ... a patient observer. This soul though, roams the world by day and streams in by night, one silken strand after another, sometimes even a tangled mess. A poet's chase—to gather the wily threads just a moment before that wispy silk turns into candy floss ... twirl them around a tethering stick and offer it as a poem to melt on your tongue ... such is the craft.

Abhijita Kulshrestha lives in Bangalore and leads an interesting life—romancing the planets and precious gemstones as a Vedic astrologer by day. And courts the written word at night!